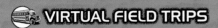

VIRTUAL FIELD TRIPS

INDEPENDENCE NATIONAL HISTORICAL PARK

A MyReportLinks.com Book

Karen Clemens Warrick

MyReportLinks.com Books

an imprint of

 Enslow Publishers, Inc.

Box 398, 40 Industrial Road
Berkeley Heights, NJ 07922
USA

MyReportLinks.com Books, an imprint of Enslow Publishers, Inc. MyReportLinks® is a registered trademark of Enslow Publishers, Inc.

Library of Congress Cataloging-in-Publication Data

Warrick, Karen Clemens.
    Independence National Historical Park / Karen Clemens Warrick.
      p. cm.
    Includes bibliographical references and index.
    ISBN 0-7660-5224-9
    1. Independence National Historical Park (Philadelphia, Pa.)—Juvenile literature. 2. Philadelphia (Pa.)—History—Revolution, 1775–1783—Juvenile literature. 3. United States—History—Revolution, 1775–1783—Juvenile literature. I. Title.
    F158.65.I3W37 2004
    974.8'11—dc22

                        2004004845

Printed in the United States of America

10 9 8 7 6 5 4 3 2 1

To Our Readers:
Through the purchase of this book, you and your library gain access to the Report Links that specifically back up this book.
The Publisher will provide access to the Report Links that back up this book and will keep these Report Links up to date on www.myreportlinks.com for five years from the book's first publication date.
We have done our best to make sure all Internet addresses in this book were active and appropriate when we went to press. However, the author and the Publisher have no control over, and assume no liability for, the material available on those Internet sites or on other Web sites they may link to.
The usage of the MyReportLinks.com Books Web site is subject to the terms and conditions stated on the Usage Policy Statement on www.myreportlinks.com.
A password may be required to access the Report Links that back up this book. The password is found on the bottom of page 4 of this book.
Any comments or suggestions can be sent by e-mail to comments@myreportlinks.com or to the address on the back cover.

MyReportLinks.com Books
Great Books, Great Links, Great for Research!

The Internet sites listed on the next four pages can save you hours of research time. These Internet sites—we call them "Report Links"—are constantly changing, but we keep them up to date on our Web site.

Give it a try! Type http://www.myreportlinks.com into your browser, click on the series title, then the book title, and scroll down to the Report Links listed for this book.

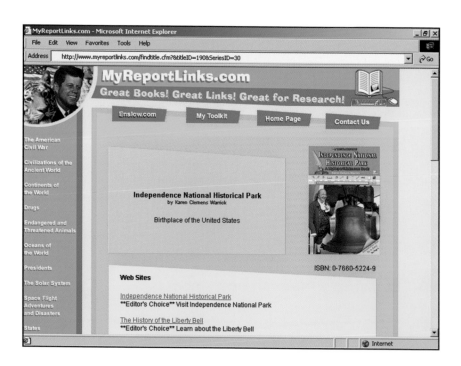

The Report Links will bring you to great source documents, photographs, and illustrations. MyReportLinks.com Books save you time, feature Report Links that are kept up to date, and make report writing easier than ever!

Please see "To Our Readers" on the copyright page for important information about this book, the MyReportLinks.com Web site, and the Report Links that back up this book.

Please enter **FTI1686** if asked for a password.

The Internet sites described below can be accessed at http://www.myreportlinks.com

*EDITOR'S CHOICE

▶**Independence National Historical Park**
At the National Park Service Web site there is a brief description of Independence National Historical Park. Click on "In Depth" to learn more.

*EDITOR'S CHOICE

▶**The History of the Liberty Bell**
Learn about the casting of the Liberty Bell, the message engraved on the bell, places the Liberty Bell has traveled to, and more.

*EDITOR'S CHOICE

▶**Independence National Historical Park: NPS Museum Collections**
At the National Park Service Web site you will view an exhibit dedicated to Independence National Historical Park.

*EDITOR'S CHOICE

▶**The Constitutional Walking Tour of Philadelphia**
Take a virtual walking tour of Philadelphia's historic locations, including the Liberty Bell, Independence Hall, and many more.

*EDITOR'S CHOICE

▶**Benjamin Franklin: Glimpses of the Man**
Learn about Benjamin Franklin's many accomplishments as an inventor, statesman, printer, and philosopher. He succeeded in other pursuits as well.

*EDITOR'S CHOICE

▶**The American Revolution**
This National Park Service Web site explores the American Revolution through virtual tours, time lines, and other resources.

Report Links

**The Internet sites described below can be accessed at
http://www.myreportlinks.com**

▶ **The Adams Papers**

At the Adams Papers Web site you can explore the life of John Adams, a time line of important events in his life, and quotations. Adams served as vice president and president while Philadelphia was still the nation's capital.

▶ **Articles of Confederation**

At the Yale Avalon Project Web site you can read the Articles of Confederation.

▶ **Benjamin Franklin**

Benjamin Franklin was born in Boston but is well-known for his time spent in Philadelphia. This PBS Web site lets the reader explore the life of Ben Franklin and his many accomplishments.

▶ **The Charters of Freedom "A New World Is At Hand"**

From the National Archives Web site you can learn about the Declaration of Independence and other historic documents.

▶ **Declaring Independence: Drafting the Documents**

Explore the Declaration of Independence, the drafting of the documents, and much more at this Library of Congress Web site.

▶ **Documents of the Continental Congress
and the Constitutional Convention**

At this Library of Congress Web site you can explore documents and images from the Continental Congress and Constitutional Convention.

▶ **Eleven Most Endangered Places**

At the National Trust for Historic Preservation you will learn why the Liberty Bell is considered an endangered historic site.

▶ **Explore the States: Pennsylvania**

America's Story From America's Library, a Library of Congress Web site, examines the history of Pennsylvania.

Any comments? Contact us: **comments@myreportlinks.com**

Report Links

The Internet sites described below can be accessed at http://www.myreportlinks.com

▶**France Allied with American Colonies February 6, 1778**

Learn the story of how Benjamin Franklin signed the Treaty of Amity and Commerce and the Treaty of Alliance. These actions brought France into the Revolutionary War on the side of the colonists.

▶**George Washington: A National Treasure**

At the George Washington: A National Treasure Web site you can learn about Gilbert Stuart's portrait of George Washington, the history of the painting, and much more.

▶**Historical Philadelphia Walk**

At the *National Geographic* Web site you can take a virtual walking tour of historic Philadelphia. Destinations include Independence National Historical Park and many other locations.

▶**Independence National Historical Park**

At the National Park Service Web site you will find an overview of Independence National Historical Park.

▶**Liberty! The American Revolution**

PBS allows you to explore the American Revolution and how it relates to the Liberty Bell.

▶**The Liberty Bell: From Obscurity to Icon**

At this National Park Web site you will learn about the Liberty Bell, the origins of its crack, and the city of Philadelphia.

▶**Liberty Bell Memorial Museum**

The Liberty Bell Memorial Museum provides facts about the Liberty Bell, a time line, and a virtual tour of the museum.

▶**9.11.01 Remembrance: Independence National Historical Park**

Learn about sites that were protected after September 11, 2001, including Independence National Historical Park.

Report Links

The Internet sites described below can be accessed at http://www.myreportlinks.com

▶**Pennsylvania**

From Infoplease.com you will learn about Pennsylvania's history and the historical significance of Pennsylvania landmarks.

▶**Rediscovering George Washington**

Learn about George Washington and his life at this Web site. You will also find documents, writings, and much more.

▶**Richard Henry Lee**

Read about Richard Henry Lee, the man whose speech to the Second Continental Congress on June 7, 1776, led the lawmakers to create the Declaration of Independence.

▶**Second Bank of the United States**

Learn about Independence National Historical Park's design, construction, architectural significance, and history.

▶*The Story Behind the Creation of Independence National Historical Park*

At this Web site you can read *The Story Behind the Creation of Independence National Historical Park*. You will learn about the Liberty Bell, Society Hill, and much more.

▶**Thomas Jefferson**

At this PBS Web site you will find a brief description of Thomas Jefferson and his contributions to American history.

▶**Today In History: The Articles of Confederation**

Today In History, a Library of Congress Web site, tells the story of the day the Continental Congress adopted the Articles of Confederation.

▶**William Penn**

This Web site provides information about William Penn. Here you will learn about the life of William Penn and his contributions to the colony of Pennsylvania.

Any comments? Contact us: **comments@myreportlinks.com**

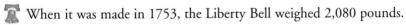
- When it was made in 1753, the Liberty Bell weighed 2,080 pounds.

- Colonists hid the Liberty Bell in 1777. They took it to Allentown, Pennsylvania. They did not want the British Army to melt it down to make cannonballs.

- At Carpenters' Hall, you can still see a weather vane filled with bullet holes. In 1777, it sat on top of the building. British Redcoats used the metal ball for target practice.

- After the Declaration of Independence was signed in Philadelphia, Benjamin Franklin said: "Gentlemen, we must now all hang together, or we shall most assuredly all hang separately."[1]

- The Free Quaker Meeting House is one park site. Most Quakers did not believe in fighting. This group declared its own independence before the Revolutionary War. They supported the war against Great Britain.

- There were many printers in Philadelphia in 1776. Benjamin Franklin was one of them. These printers often printed pamphlets speaking out against British rules.

- The post office at Franklin Court is the only one in the United States that does not fly an American flag. This is because it existed before the Revolutionary War.

- Ben Franklin wanted the wild turkey, not the bald eagle, to be the national bird.

- George Washington sat in a special chair during the Constitutional Convention. There was a sun carved on its back. At the end of the convention, Benjamin Franklin said: "I have often . . . looked at that [the sun] . . . without being able to tell whether it was rising or setting. But now . . . I have the happiness to know that it is a rising and not a setting sun."[2]

- Philadelphia was the nation's capital from 1790 to 1800. Both George Washington and John Adams took the oath for the office of president in Congress Hall.

- To begin the restoration of Independence Hall, researchers studied almost 2 million papers and books. They wanted to learn everything they could about how Independence Hall looked in 1776.

- Park visitors can tour Bishop White's house. It was one of the first homes in the city to have an indoor "necessity"—a toilet.

- The park had over 2.7 million visitors in 2003.[3] Many people come to see the Liberty Bell and Independence Hall.

Let Freedom Ring

Welcome to Independence National Historical Park. It is located in Philadelphia, Pennsylvania. The park sits near the Delaware River in the oldest part of the city. It covers several square blocks. There are many old buildings and sites to visit. These places played an important part in the birth of the United States of America.

People who lived in Philadelphia knew this area was important. By 1850, they had restored Independence Hall and Congress Hall. On the outside, both buildings looked much as

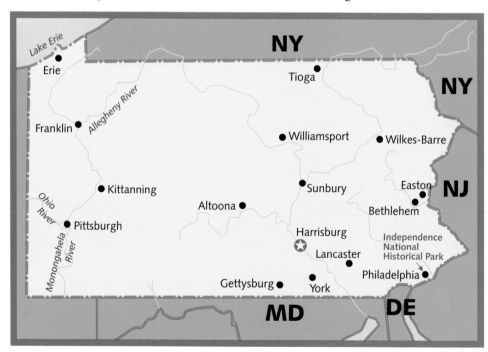

▲ *Independence National Historical Park is located in the city of Philadelphia, in Southeastern Pennsylvania, along the Delaware River.*

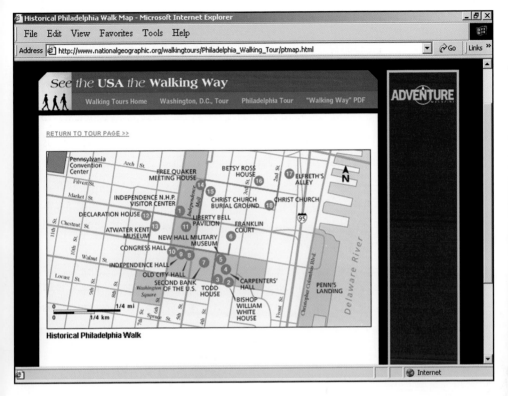

Historical Philadelphia Walk

🔺 *A visit to Philadelphia is incomplete without a tour of Independence National Historical Park.*

they had in 1776. That was when the thirteen colonies declared their independence from Great Britain.

Independence Hall became a museum. It was also the home of the Liberty Bell. During 1876, many Americans visited the old hall. They were celebrating the one hundredth anniversary of the signing of the Declaration of Independence.

Unfortunately, many other old buildings had not been cared for. In the 1940s, a group of people called the Independence Hall Association came up with a plan. Their plan would protect Independence Hall, Congress Hall, Old City Hall, and Carpenters' Hall. They wanted sites in the oldest part of the city to be preserved as a national park. They worked to convince Congress and the rest of country that it was a good idea.

Finally, the group's hard work paid off. In June 1948, Congress passed a special act. It created Independence National Historical Park. Eight years later, the park opened on July 4, 1956. Today, families can step back in time. They can stroll around Independence Mall and learn more about how the United States won its freedom.

The Liberty Bell

The Liberty Bell is one of the park's most popular exhibits. It was first called the State House Bell. The Pennsylvania Assembly ordered the bell to celebrate the fiftieth anniversary of the colony's charter. King Charles II of England had given a charter to William Penn. Penn planned the colony's government. He decided to let citizens make some of their own laws. He also allowed them to

▲ After the Civil War, the Liberty Bell was taken around the United States. People felt this would help reunify the country. This picture was taken in 1903.

choose the religion they wanted to practice. Colonists were proud of these freedoms—these liberties.

The bell was made in England. It arrived in Philadelphia on September 1, 1752. The first time someone rang the bell, it cracked. The speaker of the assembly wrote, "I had the mortification [the embarrassment] to hear that it was cracked by a stroke of the clapper . . . as it was hung up to try the sound."[1]

Two local men, John Pass and John Stow, melted down the cracked bell and made a new one. They added more copper to the metal mixture to make it stronger.

When the new bell was tried out, it did not crack, but no one liked the sound of it. So Pass and Stow recreated the bell a second time. Finally, on June 11, 1753, the new bell was hung in the steeple of the Pennsylvania State House.

The bell called the Assembly to meetings. It also called people together to hear special announcements. The bell rang out on July 8, 1776. Citizens hurried to the yard behind the State House. This was a very important day. As everyone listened, the Declaration of Independence was read for the first time.

A Famous Crack

By 1846, people noticed that the sound of the Liberty Bell's ring had changed. This was due to a thin crack in the bell. That same year, the bell was repaired and was rung during a celebration for George Washington's birthday. However, at some point during or after the celebration, the Liberty Bell cracked again and has not been rung since.[2]

When the National Park Service tried to find out why the bell had cracked, it found that the bell was worn out. It is believed that the crack started with a small defect that grew larger and larger.

Today millions of visitors go to see the bell each year. The Liberty Bell is famous for its crack. Many stoop down and peek up inside the bell. They study the spider-like metal frame that keeps the crack from getting longer.

▷ A New Name

The old State House Bell got a new name in the 1830s. A group of people called abolitionists wanted to outlaw slavery. They remembered the Bible verse on the bell. It read, "Proclaim LIBERTY throughout all the Land unto all the inhabitants thereof."[3] This group thought everyone should be free. The abolitionists printed the bell's picture on antislavery pamphlets. They gave the bell its new name—the Liberty Bell.

Shortly after the Civil War in 1865, the Thirteenth Amendment ended slavery in the United States. Many hoped the Liberty Bell would reunite the North and South. They hoped the bell would remind Americans of the Revolution. Remembering a time when Americans had fought together, and won independence from Great Britain, might create feelings of patriotism.

The bell traveled around the country. It was first sent to New Orleans, Louisiana, then to Chicago, Illinois. The bell made stops in Atlanta, Georgia; Charleston, South Carolina; and St. Louis,

▲ This replica of the Liberty Bell sits on the grounds of St. John's College in Annapolis, Maryland. It is one of fifty-five reproductions made in 1950 by the U.S. Department of the Treasury as part of a defense bond drive.

▲ *A guard watches over the Liberty Bell as visitors admire it. In 2003, the Liberty Bell was moved to a new glass-enclosed location.*

Missouri. It was in Boston, Massachusetts, for the 128th anniversary of the Battle of Bunker Hill. It also traveled cross-country to San Francisco, California. The bell drew large crowds. Its travels ended when the crack seemed to be growing. Since 1915, the Liberty Bell's home has been in Philadelphia.

▷ A Brand-New Home

In 1976, the Liberty Bell was moved. It went from Independence Hall to a building of its own on the park mall. The bell was placed in a plate glass enclosure. Beyond the bell, visitors could see Independence Hall. The hall sat in the shadow of a modern high-rise office building. Many thought that this was not the best setting for the Liberty Bell. Plans were designed for a new building.

On October 9, 2003, the Liberty Bell moved again. The new Liberty Bell Pavilion is on Sixth Street. A glass structure surrounds the Liberty Bell. No modern office buildings can be seen

△ *On October 9, 2003, the new Liberty Bell Pavilion was opened to the public. This National Park Service guide is educating the visitors about the history of the Liberty Bell.*

in the background. Its glass case was built at a special angle. This gives visitors a wonderful view of Independence Hall and its steeple against the sky in the distance.

The new Liberty Bell Center features this glass bell room. There is also an outdoor area with educational displays and an exhibit hall. Visitors can stroll all around this beautiful building. As they do, they learn the story of one of America's best-known symbols of freedom—the Liberty Bell.

Revolutionary Ideas

Trouble was brewing in 1774. England demanded that the American colonists pay a tax on their tea. To protest, people in Boston dressed up as American Indians and threw the tea into Boston Harbor. This is known as the Boston Tea Party. To punish the colonists, Britain passed the Coercive Acts, called the Intolerable Acts by the colonists. Most Englishmen had the right to vote on taxes. The colonists considered themselves to be Englishmen, but no one represented the colonists in Parliament. The colonists thought they were being taxed unfairly because they could not vote against the taxes.

▲ The members of the First Continental Congress met in Carpenters' Hall.

Colonial leaders decided that they had to act. They sent delegates to Philadelphia for meetings. Many of these men lodged and dined at City Tavern. Although the old tavern was torn down long ago, the park built a replica on the original site. Visitors today can have lunch or dinner at the tavern.

▷ A Meeting in Carpenters' Hall

Members of the First Continental Congress met in Carpenters' Hall. The hall was the home of one of the colonies' first craft guilds, or unions. The congress met in September and October 1774. Members held lots of debates. Then, they decided to ask the British government to protect their rights as Englishmen. At first, the colonists did not seek independence.

Patrick Henry was one of the delegates. Before the meetings ended, he planted a seed. This seed would grow into a new idea. At that time he said the differences "between Virginians, Pennsylvanians, New Yorkers, and New Englanders are no more. I am not a Virginian but an American."[1]

The members of the Carpenters' Company understood that the hall was important. It played a part in United States history. It was the meeting site of the First Continental Congress. They turned the hall into a museum in 1857.

Today, Carpenters' Hall is still owned by The Carpenters' Company of the City and County of Philadelphia. It is one of the best-preserved sites in the park. The hall looks much like it did in 1774. Visitors enter the building and walk into a large meeting room. Eight Windsor chairs sit in one corner. They were used by members of the First Continental Congress. A painting of Patrick Henry hangs on the wall. Official notes taken during the meetings and important letters written by members are also displayed.

▷ War With Great Britain

Members of the First Continental Congress hoped the king would hear their petition. Most members still wanted to be loyal British

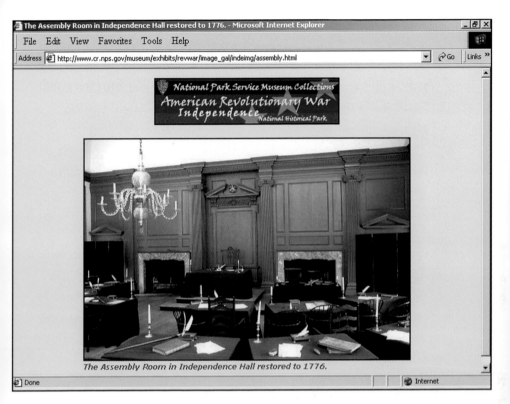

The Assembly Room in Independence Hall restored to 1776. - Microsoft Internet Explorer

File   Edit   View   Favorites   Tools   Help

Address http://www.cr.nps.gov/museum/exhibits/revwar/image_gal/indeimg/assembly.html   Go   Links

The Assembly Room in Independence Hall restored to 1776.

Done   Internet

▲ The Assembly Room of Independence Hall has been restored to what it looked like in 1776. It is in this room that George Washington was appointed commander in chief of the Continental Army, the Declaration of Independence was adopted, and the design for the first American flag was agreed upon.

subjects. However, on the morning of April 19, 1775, British Redcoats engaged the colonial militia in two separate battles. These were the Battles of Lexington and Concord, Massachusetts. No one is sure who fired first, but the Revolutionary War had begun.

Members of the First Continental Congress were called to the Second Continental Congress. They arrived in Philadelphia in May 1775. This time they met in the Assembly Room of the Pennsylvania State House. The building is now known as Independence Hall.

The delegates sat at tables covered with green, woolen cloth. The tables formed a semicircle around the speaker's platform. New Englanders sat on the north side of the room. The middle colonies took chairs on either side of the center aisle. Southerners took seats in the sunny south end of the room.

Congress needed a commander for their army. John Adams nominated George Washington, who was elected to lead the fighting force. Washington left Philadelphia immediately for Boston. He took charge of troops that had the British surrounded.

As General Washington fought the Redcoats, Congress waged its own war of words. Finally, the members began to think about independence. On June 7, 1776, Virginia delegate Richard Henry Lee made a motion. Lee declared that the thirteen American colonies should be free from British rule.

A committee was asked to draft a declaration. The declaration would explain why the colonies should be independent. Five men were assigned to this task. They were John Adams, Robert R. Livingston, Roger Sherman, Benjamin Franklin, and Thomas Jefferson.

▷ Thomas Jefferson

While serving as a delegate, Thomas Jefferson lived in rented rooms. The rooms were in the home of a German bricklayer, Jacob Graff. Jefferson had asked for a place "in the (out)skirts of the town where I may have the benefit of a freely circulating air."[2] This modest brick home was exactly what he wanted. He wrote the Declaration of Independence at his desk in the second-floor parlor. It took Jefferson two weeks to complete the first draft.

The Graff House is now called Declaration House. The home was rebuilt on its original site. Visitors must walk a few blocks from Independence Mall to see where Jefferson slept and wrote.

Adams and Franklin made a few changes to Jefferson's draft. Then the document was presented to all members of the Second Continental Congress. They made more changes.

Finally, it was time to vote for or against independence. Several Pennsylvania delegates were still not in favor of the idea. They decided not to attend the session. One Delaware delegate, Caesar

Rodney, had gone back home to help stop a riot. He rode all night so he could get back to vote. Delaware delegates would have been evenly divided without his vote.

On July 2, the votes were counted. More members voted for independence. Congress adopted Jefferson's Declaration of Independence on July 4, 1776. Four days later, the Liberty Bell (then known as the State House Bell) rang out. It called the people of the city to Independence Square. They came to hear what Congress had decided to do.

Colonel John Nixon climbed the steps to a wooden platform. He began to read from a sheet of paper. It was one of one hundred printed copies of the Declaration of Independence. The

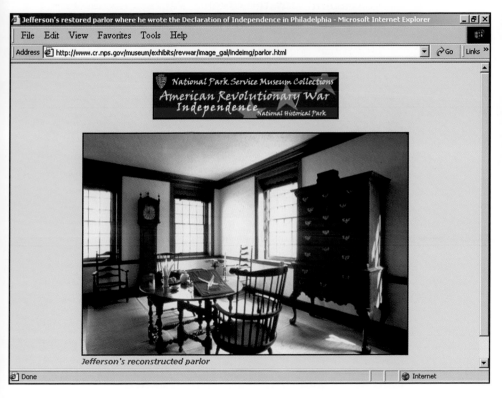

Jefferson's restored parlor where he wrote the Declaration of Independence in Philadelphia - Microsoft Internet Explorer

File   Edit   View   Favorites   Tools   Help

Address http://www.cr.nps.gov/museum/exhibits/revwar/image_gal/indeimg/parlor.html

National Park Service Museum Collections
American Revolutionary War
Independence National Historical Park

Jefferson's reconstructed parlor

△ *Jefferson's parlor, located in the Declaration House within Independence National Historical Park, is where the founding father wrote the Declaration of Independence. This house, having been torn down, was rebuilt in 1975 using old photographs as a guide.*

▲ An image of the complete Declaration of Independence.

▲ *This mural, painted by John Trumbull in 1776, was called "Declaration of Independence." It is the artist's rendition of how the signing of the Declaration may have looked.*

most important words were near the document's end: ". . . These United Colonies are, and of Right ought to be Free and Independent States."[3] Nixon finished quickly and stepped down from the platform.

Every year, park rangers reenact the first reading of the Declaration of Independence. Visitors can also read the words for themselves. The Nixon copy of the Declaration of Independence is one of the park treasures. It is on display in Independence Hall.

▷ Independence

On July 4, 1776, the Second Continental Congress officially adopted the final draft of the Declaration of Independence. In its eyes, the United States became a new country. Copies of the declaration were ordered a few days later. On August 2, members lined up to sign the document. John Hancock was the first to dip his quill pen into the silver inkstand. Hancock wrote his name in big, bold letters. He wanted to be sure that England's King George III could read his signature without glasses.

Building a New Nation

For the next year, Congress met in Independence Hall. Then on September 11, 1777, the British defeated George Washington at the Battle of the Brandywine. The battlefield was only a few miles from Philadelphia. The British marched into the city. Congress was forced to flee to Lancaster, Pennsylvania.

In April, France joined the war on the side of the United States. The British Army pulled out of Philadelphia. They marched to New York City. There they prepared for the French fleet to attack. Congress returned to Philadelphia.

▲ This memorial is called Tomb of the Unknown Soldier of the Revolution. It is located in Washington Square, across from Independence Mall.

The Revolutionary War lasted from 1775 until 1783. The final battle was fought at Yorktown, Virginia. Washington and the French surrounded British General Charles Cornwallis. The attack lasted for weeks. Soon the Redcoats were almost out of food and ammunition.

The battle ended on October 19, 1781. Cornwallis raised a white flag. He surrendered with eight thousand soldiers. The Treaty of Paris was signed on September 3, 1783. That officially ended the war and made the United States an independent country.

Problems with the Articles of Confederation

Shortly after the Treaty of Paris was signed, the United States faced some problems. Its new government was not working. The Second Continental Congress had drafted a document with thirteen articles. It was called the Articles of Confederation. The country had worked under this plan since 1781.

In February 1786, Virginia Governor Patrick Henry called a meeting. He invited all the other governors to send delegates to Annapolis, Maryland. These delegates asked for a Constitutional Convention. They sent their request to Congress. The request was granted.

The Constitutional Convention

The Constitutional Convention was held in Independence Hall. Meetings began on May 25, 1787. George Washington and Benjamin Franklin were asked to lead the convention. Eighty-two-year-old Franklin's health was poor. He asked Washington to accept the job.

That summer, delegates discussed the issues. They decided that the legislature should have two houses. It took much longer to decide how many representatives each state should have. The debate over this issue was heated. It nearly ended the meetings before all the work was finished.

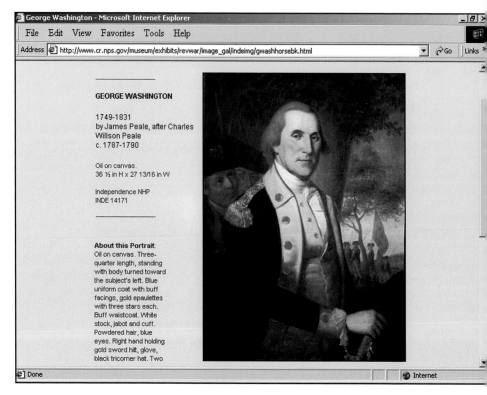

GEORGE WASHINGTON

1749-1831
by James Peale, after Charles
Willson Peale
c. 1787-1790

Oil on canvas.
36 ½ in H x 27 13/16 in W

Independence NHP
INDE 14171

About this Portrait:
Oil on canvas. Three-
quarter length, standing
with body turned toward
the subject's left. Blue
uniform coat with buff
facings, gold epaulettes
with three stars each.
Buff waistcoat. White
stock, jabot and cuff.
Powdered hair, blue
eyes. Right hand holding
gold sword hilt, glove,
black tricorner hat. Two

▲ *This portrait of George Washington was painted circa 1790 by James Peale.*
The artist's brother, Charles Willson Peale, collected portraits during this era,
ninety-four of which are in Independence National Historical Park collections.

Finally, one member suggested a plan. In this plan, members would be elected to the House of Representatives based on the state's population. In the other house, the Senate, each state would have two representatives. This plan is remembered as the "Great Compromise."

After four months of debate and compromise, members of the Constitutional Convention finished their work. No one was happy with everything in the final plan. Everyone had to give up something. The founding fathers had compromised to create a new government for the country.

On September 17, 1787, members dipped quills into a silver inkstand. It was the same one used to sign the Declaration of

Independence. Washington was the first in line. Then other members signed the Constitution of the United States.

▷ Philadelphia, the Nation's Capital

George Washington became the country's first president. Congress planned a new capital city. Washington D.C., would take ten years to build. Meanwhile, Philadelphia would be the country's capital.

Two public buildings had been built on either side of the Pennsylvania State House: the County Court House and City Hall. Both buildings were offered to the United States government.

On December 6, 1790, the United States Congress held its first meetings in the County Court House. Sixty-five representatives went to work. Vice President John Adams presided over the twenty-six senators. The building was soon renamed Congress Hall.

Old City Hall

Congress Hall

▲ *This engraving of the Pennsylvania State House (now Independence Hall) shows what the buildings may have looked like in colonial times. Old City Hall is located on one side of Independence Hall, and Congress Hall sits on the other side.*

Today, visitors enter Congress Hall from the east side. They walk into the building just as representatives did in 1790. The hall is a two-story brick building with a large bay in the rear. The rooms inside had been designed as courtrooms. They were remodeled for Congress to use. The floors were carpeted. Stoves replaced fireplaces. The House of Representatives met in the large room on the first floor. Senate meetings were held upstairs.

Old City Hall sits on the east side of Independence Hall. The Supreme Court held sessions there. During those ten years, the court's role in government was established. The Supreme Court became the interpreter of the Constitution. Inside the building, visitors today can watch a short film. It explains how the country's judicial system developed.

▷ Independence Hall Today

Independence Hall is one of the best-known buildings in the United States today. As visitors walk across Independence Square, they admire its beautiful brick walls and gaze up at its bell tower. The hall is a permanent reminder of what happened there more than two hundred years ago.

The Old State House, now Independence Hall, was built between 1732 and 1736. It was built for the Pennsylvania State Assembly. A bell tower was added in 1751. Over the years, the old building was remodeled again and again. In the 1820s, there was even talk of tearing it down. Fortunately, that did not happen.

Philadelphia gave Independence Hall to the National Park Service on January 2, 1951. The building was run down. It needed many repairs. There were leaks in the roof. The brick walls and wooden trim had to be fixed.

The park staff set to work immediately. They wanted to have the hall in order by the first week in July. That was when they planned to hold a ceremony. It would celebrate the 175th anniversary of the signing of the Declaration of Independence. The outside and inside of the building were painted. New treads

▲ The renovations on Independence Hall were completed in 1972. The statue in front of the building is of Commodore John Barry, a naval commander during the Revolutionary War.

were put in the great tower stairs. The roof, walls, and trims were mended.

This was only the beginning of the work that needed to be done. Next, the staff began to do research. They wanted to restore Independence Hall to make it look like it had in 1776. They needed lots of information. The staff searched for plans that told them what the building was like inside and out. They tried to learn all about its furniture and wall hangings. They also studied the events that had taken place within its walls and on its grounds.

To pay for the restoration project, park planners asked American citizens to make donations. The campaign was successful. By August 2, 1954, they had raised more than two hundred thousand dollars for the project. The restoration of Independence Hall took over twenty years. In 1972, the building was completed inside and out.

Today, visitors to Independence Hall can tour the Assembly Room. They see the place where members debated the Declaration of Independence and the Constitution. Green cloths cover tables like the ones members sat around. A candle chandelier hangs from the ceiling. It provided light to work by. The silver inkstand used to sign both documents is on display. One of the most treasured pieces in the park's collection is here. It is the high-backed chair used by George Washington. A rising sun is carved on its wooden back.

All the park's careful research and hard work paid off. A visit today to Independence Hall takes visitors back to 1776. As they open the door, they begin a walk back in time. Visitors can see the history of the founding fathers at work, creating a new and independent country.

Benjamin Franklin: Philadelphia Citizen

In October 1723, Benjamin Franklin arrived in Philadelphia. He stepped from a boat he had helped row up the Delaware River. Then, the young man walked up Market Street. "I was dirty from my journey; my pockets were stuffed out with shirts and stockings, and I knew no soul nor where to look for lodging." He wrote later, "I was fatigued [tired] with travelling, rowing, and . . . very hungry, and my whole stock of cash consisted of a Dutch dollar and about a shilling in copper."[1]

Franklin was seventeen years old. He had left his home in Boston. He had run away from his job as a printer's apprentice. No one who saw him could have guessed that some day Franklin would be Philadelphia's most famous citizen.

▶ The Printer

Franklin soon found a job working for a printer

This lithograph of Benjamin ▶ Franklin was created in the 1840s. It depicts Franklin in his upper-middle age years.

in the city. He worked hard. He learned everything he could about writing and how to run a print shop. At twenty-four, he opened his own shop and started his own newspaper, *The Pennsylvania Gazette*. People in Philadelphia enjoyed the articles and funny letters that Franklin wrote.

Franklin published an almanac from 1733 until 1758. It was called *Poor Richard's Almanack*. He wrote under the pen name Richard Saunders. Franklin's witty voice made this almanac special. He included famous sayings such as, "early to bed, early to rise makes a man healthy, wealthy, and wise." The first copies sold out quickly. Orders poured in from all over. Soon the name of Benjamin Franklin was known throughout the thirteen English colonies.

Today, park visitors can tour the Franklin Court Printing Office. Inside they will see what a colonial print shop looked like. Franklin built the shop for his grandson, Benjamin Franklin Bache.

A Community Leader and Inventor

Franklin turned his print shop into a successful business. Then he worked on public projects for several years. Franklin was proudest of one project in particular. It was a lending library. The Library Company of Philadelphia was founded in 1731. That makes it the oldest subscription library in America today. Friends helped Franklin work on this project. Everyone donated books they owned. Anyone could visit the room and look at the books, but only members could borrow them. The original library building was torn down in 1884. Today, visitors can see a replica built on park land. It is owned by the American Philosophical Society. This group had helped Franklin start the library so many years ago. They take care of it today.

Colonial Postmaster

In 1737, Franklin took another job—deputy postmaster of Philadelphia. In 1753, he left this post and took a position as

The Franklin Court Printing Office is located down the road from Independence Mall, between Chestnut and Market streets. Benjamin Franklin first became well-known for his printing businesses.

deputy postmaster general of North America. His job was to oversee postal delivery in the thirteen colonies. Franklin made plans to improve mail delivery.

Franklin visited all the post offices in the northern colonies. He studied the roads over which mail was carried. He selected the best routes so that mail would arrive as expected. Mail service grew more dependable. More people began to send letters by post. Franklin's improvements helped pull "the scattered colonies together."[2]

Today, visitors can tour the B. Free Franklin Post Office and Museum. The reconstructed post office is located at 316 Market Street. It was built on the site of Franklin's wife's family home.

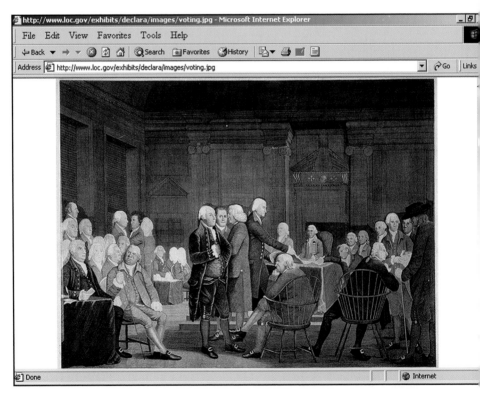

▲ This unfinished 1776 engraving entitled Congress shows Thomas Jefferson submitting his committee's draft of the Declaration of Independence to the Second Continental Congress. The engraving was done by Edward Savage after a painting by Robert Edge Pine. Benjamin Franklin is seated in the center.

Franklin Court - Microsoft Internet Explorer

File   Edit   View   Favorites   Tools   Help

Address http://www.nps.gov/inde/Franklin_Court/Pages/318.html   Go

Franklin Court
318 Market

Franklin's Life   Urban Archaeology   Material Culture

Information   Urban Landscape   Kids Corner

Welcome to 318 Market Street

Originally owned by Benjamin Franklin, the former tenant house at 318 Market Street is a unique museum that reveals more than Benjamin Franklin's history. Unlike most house museums, 318 Market does not represent a specific moment in history or one family's experience within the house and the city. The walls of the house have been stripped

Internet

▲ *The building at 318 Market Street was once owned by Benjamin Franklin. Now the building is a museum.*

▷ The Founding Father

When trouble grew between the thirteen colonies and Great Britain, Franklin took an active role. He was one of the first to believe independence was the only answer. It earned him the title "Father of the Revolution."[3]

Franklin was sixty-nine years old when the Second Continental Congress gathered in Independence Hall. He wrote a plan for the new government. It was the first plan adopted by the thirteen states. He designed the United States' paper currency. He helped create the Great Seal, which features an eagle on one side and a pyramid on the other. The seal was printed on all official documents. Franklin also helped edit the Declaration of Independence.

▲ This statue of Benjamin Franklin is located at the entrance to the Franklin Institute in Philadelphia. Franklin played a large role in shaping the history of the city of Philadelphia as well as the United States.

After all that, the elderly man still had more to do. He sailed to France. He won that country's support for the thirteen colonies in the American Revolution. The French Army and Navy sent ships and soldiers. Many believe the war would have been lost without France's help. When the war ended, Franklin also helped negotiate the treaty with Great Britain. He arrived home on September 14, 1785. He stepped off a ship at the Market Street wharf. Church bells rang and guns were fired in tribute for all he had done.

Oldest Member of the Constitutional Convention

By 1787, Franklin's health was poor. He still took on another task to help the country. He was a member of the Constitutional Convention. Meetings were again held in Independence Hall.

For four months the members debated the issues. They had to make many compromises. Finally, they settled on a plan. Franklin offered a comment before members voted. He reminded the convention that this document was not perfect. Yet he believed that it was as perfect as they could make it. He knew that no other convention could have done a better job. The Constitution went into effect on June 21, 1788.

Benjamin Franklin died two years after the Constitutional Convention completed its job. He died on April 17, 1790, at the age of eighty-four. He was buried beside his wife, Deborah. Their graves can be found in the Christ Church cemetery.

Franklin Court Today

We meet many founding fathers briefly on a visit to the park. Many have monuments dedicated to them. You can visit memorials for George Washington and Thomas Jefferson in the country's early capital city. You can also tour homes of both men.

However, in Philadelphia, little was left to help remember its most famous citizen. Franklin's grandchildren tore down his house. It was the one he had designed and built for his wife and daughter. The park service decided to build a memorial for Benjamin Franklin. This became a major purpose of the park.

Franklin Court is located along Market Street where Franklin had built a home. It took two years to complete. Then his wife, Deborah, and their daughter, Sally, moved in. Franklin was in London at the time. After he returned to Philadelphia in 1785, Franklin lived in the house until his death.

The park hoped to restore the house but could not find a picture of the building. They decided instead to create a "ghost" structure. Steel beams outline the walls and roof. Coloring in the pavement shows the floor plan of the house and shop. Paths, bushes, and flowers hint at how the garden might have looked. There is even a shady mulberry tree like the one Franklin enjoyed sitting under.

At the west side of the court, an entrance leads down a long ramp to an underground museum. Inside, visitors can see objects that belonged to Franklin or are like those he used. Displays around the room tell about all he accomplished. The museum also features a film about his family life. You get to know Franklin—the community leader, the printer, and the inventor.

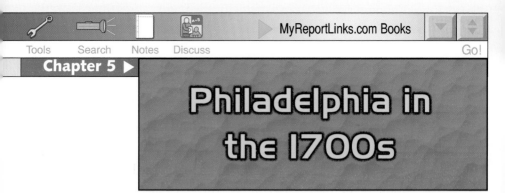

Philadelphia in the 1700s

William Penn founded Philadelphia in 1682. He built the city on the Delaware River near a good harbor. Penn founded his city for a special reason: he and his friends wanted religious freedom. Penn was a Quaker, and this religious group was not popular in England. Many Quakers moved to Philadelphia. They believed

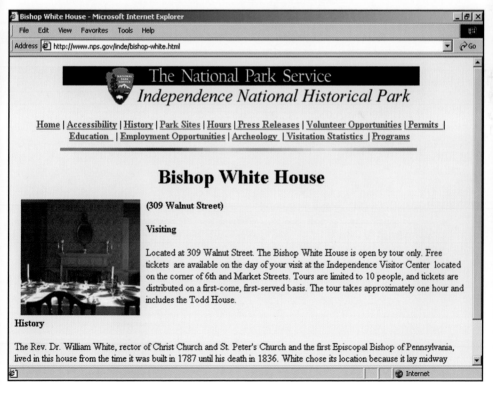

The Bishop White House is one of the many historical attractions at Independence National Historical Park.

▲ Horse-drawn carriages line the streets around Independence Mall. The carriages give visitors a feel for what Philadelphia may have been like in Revolutionary times.

everyone should be free to worship as they pleased. Thanks to Penn, many colonists began to enjoy religious freedom.

Four sites in the park today are churches. All are open to the public. Christ Church was built between 1727 and 1754. George Washington and Benjamin Franklin attended services there. Visitors today can see the pews where both men sat with their families. Franklin and his wife, Deborah, are buried in the Christ Church cemetery. The Franklin graves can be seen through the fence.

Visitors can also tour the home of Bishop William White. He was an important church official. He lived in the city after the United States won its independence. His home shows how well-to-do people lived during that time.

People moved to Philadelphia for religious freedom. They also came for other reasons. The city was clean and modern. Most streets were paved with brick and cleaned often. In the 1700s, Philadelphia was a model for other cities.

The park wanted to honor the city's founder. They built Welcome Park on the site of Penn's home. The home was called the Slate Roof House. He lived there from 1699 to 1701. In Welcome Park, visitors can see the original plans for Penn's city. The design is imprinted in the pavement. In its center, there is a statue of William Penn. Murals on a wall bordering the park tell you more about the man described by Thomas Jefferson as "the greatest law-giver the world has produced."

▷ During the War for Independence

By 1776, nearly thirty thousand people lived in Philadelphia. There were more than six thousand houses and about three hundred shops. It was one of the largest cities in the British Empire. Many immigrants moved to Penn's city. They came from England, Germany, Scotland, and Ireland. They planned to make a better life for their families in Philadelphia.

The city was an important seaport. Many people worked in the shipping industry. Goods from around the world were brought into the harbor. In addition to cargo, ships also brought people who brought new ideas to Philadelphia. People in the city were interested in science, painting, and music. They built libraries and started discussion clubs. They worked on projects to improve the city. Schools were opened for young people. All this made the city an attractive place to live.

People in the city were also excited by new ideas. This attitude made the city a good place to discuss building a new country. It was the perfect site for members of the Continental Congress and Constitutional Convention to work.

The Capital City

By 1790, Philadelphia was America's most important city. It was also the country's trade center. It soon became even more important. For ten years (1790–1800), Philadelphia was the capital of the United States. The city continued to grow during this decade. It became a center for banking. More and more ships sailed in and out of the harbor. They brought goods of all kinds to the city. Shops in the city also made goods. They built wagons, made fine silver, and stitched clothes like the products people could buy in Europe. Philadelphians could make a good living. Many lived very comfortably.

To learn more about how families lived during this time, visitors can tour two homes in the park. President George Washington lived in the Deshler-Morris House. It is the oldest house still standing that a president lived in in the United States.

David Deshler built the house during parts of 1772 and 1773. He was a Quaker merchant. During the Revolutionary War, the British seized the house. General Sir William Howe used it as his headquarters. Years later, the Morris family bought the house. They lived there for over one hundred years. In 1948, the family decided to donate the home to the National Park Service.

People from all over the world come to Philadelphia and walk down the cobblestone streets around Independence National Historical Park.

Visitors may also want to tour the Todd House. It was built in 1775. Lawyer John Todd and his wife, Dolley Payne, lived there. John Todd died in 1793. After his death, Dolley remarried. Her second husband was James Madison. Madison became the fourth president of the United States. The Todd House shows visitors an example of how the middle class lived during the years that Philadelphia was the country's capital.

A Symbol of Independence Today

A visit to Independence National Historical Park tells a story. That story covers more than one hundred years. It begins when William Penn founded his city on the Delaware River. The story ends when the United States government moved to its new capital city, Washington, D.C. In between, exciting and important events in the history of the United States took place.

In 1776, the founding fathers met inside Independence Hall. They dreamed of a free country. The Declaration of Independence was a major step in making that dream a reality. Nine years later, the Constitutional Convention debated and compromised on many issues. They wanted to create a new kind of government. Their hard work paid off. The seed they planted in 1787 grew into the United States of America. Today it is the world's oldest republic, a model for other nations.

This national park attracts many visitors. They come from all fifty states and from countries around the world. They come to see Independence Hall and the Liberty Bell. They walk through Franklin Court, Welcome Park, and the Todd House. They learn about the people who lived during the 1700s. Visitors also learn the story of how thirteen British colonies won their independence. They discover that many milestones took place in old Philadelphia—in an area now known as Independence National Historical Park.

Glossary

Articles of Confederation—A governing agreement adopted in 1781 by representatives of each of the thirteen colonies that established the United States federal government.

colony—A territory that is a separate land from a parent country but still is ruled by the parent country.

Congress—A term used to refer to the members of both the U.S. House of Representatives and Senate.

Constitutional Convention—A meeting of United States lawmakers held in 1787 to talk about strengthening the Articles of Confederation. The members of the convention eventually drafted the United States Constitution.

Continental Congress—A meeting held in Philadelphia of representatives from each of the American colonies. The First Continental Congress met in September 1774, and the Second Continental Congress met in April 1775. The second meeting produced the Declaration of Independence.

ghost structure—An unfinished building that is used as an architectural example.

militia—A group of citizens organized for military service that is not the official army of the land. This is usually a volunteer force.

National Park Service—Established in 1916, it is part of the U.S. Department of the Interior. It manages all of the national parks and landmarks.

New England—The area of the Northeastern United States which includes the states of Connecticut, Maine, Massachusetts, New Hampshire, Rhode Island, and Vermont.

postmaster—One who is in charge of a post office or many post offices.

Redcoats—A name given to British troops because they wore bright red jackets.

religious freedom—The right of people to believe and worship any religion they like without worrying that others will punish them for their beliefs.

replica—An exact copy of something.

restoration—The act of making something look or work exactly as it did before.

statesman—A man who works in government.

Independence National Historical Park Facts

1. Esmond Wright, *Franklin of Philadelphia* (Boston: Harvard University Press, 1986), p. 247.

2. H. W. Brands, *The First American: The Life and Times of Benjamin Franklin* (New York: Doubleday, 2000), p. 118.

3. U.S. Department of the Interior, "Independence," n.d., <http://www.nps.gov/inde/> (June 3, 2004).

Chapter 1. Let Freedom Ring

1. Charles Michael Boland, *Ring in the Jubilee, The Epic of America's Liberty Bell* (Riverside, Conn.: The Chatham Press, Inc., 1973), p. 41.

2. National Park Service, "The Liberty Bell," *Independence National Historical Park,* n.d., <http://www.nps.gov/inde/liberty -bell.html> (August 12, 2004).

3. Boland, p. 23.

Chapter 2. Revolutionary Ideas

1. *Independence: A Guide to Independence National Historical Park* (Washington, D.C.: Division of Publications National Park Service, 1982), p. 22.

2. *Independence National Historical Park, The Story Behind the Scenery* (Las Vegas: KC Publications, 1990), p. 17.

3. "The Declaration of Independence," *Great Essentials: An Exhibition of Democracy at Independence National Historical Park,* n.d., <www.north-america.de/great_essentials.htm> (August 20, 2003).

Chapter 4. Benjamin Franklin: Philadelphia Citizen

1. Benjamin Franklin, *The Autobiography of Benjamin Franklin and Selections From His Other Writings* (New York: Carlton House, 1944), p. 27.

2. Dr. W. Cleon Skousen and Dr. M. Richard Maxfield, *The Real Ben Franklin, part II: Timeless Treasures from Benjamin Franklin* (Salt Lake City: Freemen Institute, 1982), p. 95.

3. Edwin Wildman, *The Founders of America in the Days of the Revolution* (New York: Books for Libraries Press, 1924), p. 3.

Adler, David A. *B. Franklin, Printer.* New York: Holiday House, 2001.

Britton, Tamara L. *Independence Hall.* Edina, Minn.: ABDO Publishing Co., 2003.

Cooper, Jason. *Historic Philadelphia.* Vero Beach, Fla.: Rourke Book Co., 2001.

Foster, Leila Merrell. *Benjamin Franklin.* Springfield, N.J.: Enslow Publishers, Inc., 1997.

Hess, Debra. *The Liberty Bell.* New York: Benchmark Books, 2003.

Marcovitz, Hal. *Independence Hall.* Philadelphia: Mason Crest Publishers, 2003.

McCave, Marta. *Philadelphia Access.* New York: Access Press, 1996.

Oberle, Lora Polack. *The Declaration of Independence.* Mankato, Minn.: Bridgestone Books, 2002.

O'Connell, Kim A. *Pennsylvania.* Berkeley Heights, N.J.: MyReportLinks.com Books, 2003.

Parks, Peggy. *Benjamin Franklin.* San Diego, Calif.: Blackbirch Press, 2003.

Schomp, Virginia. *The Revolutionary War.* New York: Benchmark Books, 2003.

Steen, Sandra and Susan Steen. *Independence Hall.* New York: Dillon Press, 1994.

Yanuck, Debbie L. *The Liberty Bell.* Mankato, Minn.: Capstone Press, 2003.